FORWARD

Fresh herbs are an incredibly important part of any kitchen and of my life as a chef. As a teacher of both professional chefs and home cooks, I always emphasize the use of fresh herbs and using quality ingredients. Gourmet Garden Fresh Herbs and Spices meet both of those requirements for me...and I know fresh.

When I tell people I grew up in Indiana, they automatically assume I grew up on a farm. In fact, I grew up just outside of Gary in a pretty urban area. We had a big yard but no fresh-from-the-Indiana-farm produce. That is, until my dad decided to plant an herb garden. Now, mind you, this was no window box herb garden. This was a 30 foot by 10 foot plot of every herb and spice you could grow in Northwest Indiana. Before most people in our area knew what Thai Basil was, we were growing it and using it in cooking. At a very young age, I learned what a difference fresh herbs and spices can make. So when I first tried Gourmet Garden Fresh Herbs and Spices, I was amazed at the flavor and freshness I achieved in my cooking by using them.

No more substituting dry for fresh herbs during the winter. No more garlic smell on my hands. No more stinging fingers from chopping up chilies. No more throwing away a bunch of dead cilantro because I only needed one tablespoon but had to buy an entire bunch. And more time to spend with my family and friends because these products make cooking so much faster.

Aside from teaching professional cooking, I also teach home cooks how to take their favorite foods and make delicious, healthy versions of them. Showing them, and letting them taste foods made with Gourmet Garden Herbs and Spices has literally changed some of my clients' lives just by making cooking easier and grocery shopping less overwhelming. When I change a traditionally "unhealthy" recipe into a more healthful version, two things I do right away are cut out some of the fat and salt. When you lose fat and salt, you usually lose a lot of flavor as well. So, how do I boost the flavor? Fresh herbs and spices is how. Gourmet Garden has made that so much easier for me, who is always striving not only to give people the tastiest and healthiest options, but also to eat as healthy as possible while still enjoying every bite.

Those of us who made this cookbook for you hope that you will find the same joy we had in cooking delicious meals that you can be proud of serving to your families and friends. Proud of how delicious and beautiful they are, and proud that you are nourishing their bodies with good-for-you dishes. Eat well!

-Chef Jennifer Bucko Lamplough

P.S. **Please check out the sample meal plan at the back of this book.**

CONTENTS

Cooking with Herbs and Spices

A cookbook full of flavorful, fast and healthy recipes made fresh and easy with Gourmet Garden herbs and spices.

Published by:
Botanical Food Company, Inc.
101 Parkshore Drive, Suite 100
Folsom, CA 95630
Tel. 1-888-878-3663

gourmetgarden.com
facebook.com/gourmetgarden
youtube.com/gourmetgarden

Creative Design and Layout: Adam Flissinger, Nancy Chidel
Photography: Chris Cassidy Photography, cassidyphoto.com
Food Stylist: Shannon Kinsella
Recipe development and testing: Shannon Kinsella, Jennifer Bucko Lamplough, Kari Underly*
Editor and Project Manager: Margaret Laport
Printing & Binding: Savvy Print Solutions

*Special Thanks to Kari Underly for graciously allowing us to include her Italian Herbs Chickpea Salad recipe which has quickly become a favorite.

GF = Gluten free

OUR FARMERS...

Gourmet Garden herbs start off their life as a little seed in the fertile soil of the Callide Valley in Central Queensland, Australia. They are cared for, fed and are grown organically by our farmers who are truly passionate about producing fresh herbs that are full of flavor.

Our farmers are the backbone of Gourmet Garden and provide us and you with quality herbs that are harvested at the optimum time to ensure all of the essential oils (the flavor and aroma) are captured in the leaves before being plucked from the soil.

Once the herbs are picked the race begins to keep the goodness locked in. Within 24 hours of harvest the fresh herbs are washed, chopped and blended into a paste. These delicious herbs last for three months in the fridge, meaning there's no reason not to have fresh herbs and spices at your fingertips every day. How easy is that!

BASIL

FLAVOR
Fresh basil has an initial subtle peppery flavor. The taste then evolves into a slightly sweet licorice flavor.

AROMA
Basil has a strong, pungent, sweet and somewhat menthol aroma.

COOKING & FOOD PAIRINGS
It is best to add fresh basil leaves at the very end of the cooking process or stir into dressings and soups, to preserve the delicate flavors. Sweet basil pairs beautifully with olive oil, oregano, thyme, garlic, onions, tomatoes, zucchini, bell peppers, cucumbers, pork, chicken, pasta, eggs, pizza and green leafy salads.

HEALTH BENEFITS
Studies prove that basil is a good source of antioxidants and contains more antioxidants per serving than most vegetables and many fruit so adding just a little basil to your meals can also give your diet an antioxidant boost. Eating some fresh basil leaves is reputed to help with a blocked nose! It is traditionally used for supplementary treatment of stress, asthma and diabetes in India.

GOURMET GARDEN BASIL
Each 4 oz. tube contains 3 bunches of Sweet Genovese basil and is gluten free. Find Gourmet Garden Basil in the fresh produce section of your supermarket.

RECIPES
Basil Mushroom Frittata (p18)

Cheeseless Herbed Mac and Cheese (p70)

Cioppino with Garlic, Basil and Parsley (p76)

Garlicky Spaghetti Squash Carbonara (p78)

Multigrain Spaghetti with Basil Kale Pesto (p80)

Pear and Brown Rice Salad with Basil & Garlic (p58)

Penne with Garlic, Chicken, Basil and Greens (p82)

Spanish Style Basil & Greens Gazpacho (p34)

Triple Bean Salad with Basil & Garlic (p62)

CHILI PEPPER

FLAVOR
Chili peppers come in many shapes, sizes and flavors; they can be hot, sweet, fruity, earthy, smoky and floral. As with bell peppers, the red tends to be the sweetest form.

COOKING & FOOD PAIRINGS
Chili pepper can be found in dishes from all around the globe, from Indian curries to Korean kimchee to Mexican food. Chili peppers work well with garlic, fermented beans, ginger, coconuts, shallots and fish. It can be used to balance flavors in a dish. The heat comes from slicing into the veins as well as the seeds. Try putting a whole chili into your tomato sauce to just give it a bit of flavor.

HEALTH BENEFITS
Chili peppers are an excellent way to boost your daily antioxidant intake, helping you build your body's defenses, your immune system and maximize your wellbeing. Evidence suggests capsaicin, the compound that gives chili peppers their heat, may help weight loss by triggering certain protein changes in the body that prevents fat storage. Chili pepper also contains high amounts of vitamin C and B, potassium, magnesium and iron.

GOURMET GARDEN CHILI PEPPER
Each 4 oz. tube contains a blend of 5 red cayenne and habanero chili peppers and is gluten free. Find Gourmet Garden Chili Pepper in the fresh produce section of your supermarket.

RECIPES

CILANTRO

FLAVOR
Cilantro has a distinctive, pungent earthy taste similar to a blend of lemon and sage.

AROMA
Cilantro has a refreshing, piney, slightly lemony aroma with mint and pepper overtones. Some folks detect a soapy smell, which appears to be due to a genetic component.

COOKING & FOOD PAIRING

Cilantro is best added to dishes just before serving as heat can reduce its potency. Great with chili, carrot, basil, mint, chicken, beef, avocado, coconut, couscous, garlic, ginger, soy sauce, fish, shrimp, scallops and mussels.

HEALTH BENEFITS
Traditionally, cilantro was used to treat migraines and indigestion, to help purify the blood and to relieve nausea, pain in joints and rheumatism. Researchers found that cilantro can assist with clearing the body of lead, aluminum and mercury. Cilantro contains antioxidants, which can delay or prevent the spoilage of food seasoned with this spice. It also has been found to have antibacterial properties.

GOURMET GARDEN CILANTRO
Each 4 oz. tube contains 3 bunches of chopped fresh cilantro and is gluten free. Find Gourmet Garden Cilantro in the fresh produce section of your supermarket.

RECIPES
Cabbage Salad with Ginger & Cilantro Dressing (p40)

Caribbean Turkey Burger with Chili Pepper Mayo (p68)

Chicken Quesadilla with Cilantro and Garlic (p72)

Cilantro Hummus (p28)

Cilantro Lentil Soup (p30)

Cilantro-Honey Glazed Salmon (p74)

Curry Ginger Chicken Salad (p42)

Garlicky Brussels Sprouts Slaw (p48)

Pearl Couscous with Parsley, Cilantro and Greens (p60)

Pulled Ginger-Chicken Slider with Cilantro Slaw (p84)

Slow Cooker Cilantro Shredded Beef (Ropa Vieja) (p86)

Spicy Turkey Sausage Chili with Cilantro (p88)

DILL

FLAVOR
Dill's flavor is very similar to that of caraway, but has a tangy, grassy flavor to it along with a hint of lemon, pine and fennel.

AROMA
Dill has a faint, almost similar scent of aniseed. The herb, especially when fresh, has a much sweeter fragrance than dried fruits. Dill has a wonderfully pungent aroma.

COOKING & FOOD PAIRING
Add dill to New York style smoked salmon and cream cheese bagels or use dill to add flavor to dishes that feature egg, potato and fish, such as gravlax.

HEALTH BENEFITS
Dill is usually given as dill water which is thought to aid in children's flatulence or indigestion. The main benefit from dill is calming the digestive system. The essential oil found in dill assists in relieving intestinal spasms and griping. If you suffer from a cold, dill is a fantastic cure as it is often added to cold and flu remedies.

GOURMET GARDEN DILL
Each 4 oz. tube contains 3 bunches of chopped fresh dill and is gluten free. Find Gourmet Garden Dill in the fresh produce section of your supermarket

RECIPES
Dijon Dill Potato Salad (p44)
Dill Green Bean Salad (p46)

GARLIC

FLAVOR

Garlic has a pungent, spicy flavor that mellows and sweetens considerably with cooking. While cooking softens the flavor, roasting gives garlic a well-balanced, delicate, nutty flavor.

COOKING & FOOD PAIRING

Garlic is an essential ingredient in French, Italian, Spanish and Middle Eastern cooking. Garlic is often used as a base for stir-frys, curries, soups and sauces and is often added with onions and other spices. Garlic works wonderfully when matched with onions, ginger, basil, turmeric, greens, beans, spinach, chicken, parsley, pork and seafood. Garlic has the ability to modify other flavors such as tomato, chilies, onions and ginger.

HEALTH BENEFITS

Though garlic may not always bring good luck, protect against evil or ward off vampires, it is guaranteed to clear up unwanted acne, assist with cardio vascular health, lower high cholesterol while also acting as a natural antibiotic to stimulate your immune system. It also has anti-microbial and anti-fungal properties to help with yeast infections and Athlete's foot. So next time you're cooking in the kitchen be sure to mix in some garlic to increase your daily dose of Vitamin C and help ward off "evil" diseases.

GOURMET GARDEN GARLIC OR CHUNKY GARLIC

Each 4 oz. tube contains 23 cloves chopped garlic and is gluten free. Find Gourmet Garden Garlic in the fresh produce section of your supermarket.

RECIPES

Baked Hot Wings with Bleu Cheese Parsley Dip (p26)
Barley Risotto with Italian Herbs (p66)
Basil Mushroom Frittata (p18)
Cabbage Salad with Ginger & Cilantro Dressing (p40)
Caribbean Turkey Burger with Chili Pepper Mayo (p68)
Cheeseless Herbed Mac and Cheese (p70)
Chicken Quesadilla with Cilantro and Garlic (p72)
Cilantro Hummus (p28)
Cilantro Lentil Soup (p30)
Cilantro-Honey Glazed Salmon (p74)
Cioppino with Garlic, Basil and Parsley (p76)
Curry Ginger Chicken Salad (p42)
Garlicky Brussels Sprouts Slaw (p48)
Garlicky Spaghetti Squash Carbonara (p78)
Ginger Lemon Grass Asparagus (p50)
Greek Salad with Lemon Garlic Dressing (p52)
Mixed Greens and Pears with Italian Herbs Dressing (p56)
Multigrain Spaghetti with Basil Kale Pesto (p80)
Oregano and Feta Grilled Flatbread (p32)
Pear and Brown Rice Salad with Basil & Garlic (p58)
Penne with Garlic, Chicken, Basil and Greens (p82)
Polenta Benedict with Italian Herb Yogurt "Hollandaise" (p22)
Pulled Ginger-Chicken Slider with Cilantro Slaw (p84)
Slow Cooker Cilantro Shredded Beef (Ropa Vieja) (p86)
Spanish Style Basil & Greens Gazpacho (p34)
Spicy Greens and Chickpea Soup (p36)
Spicy Turkey Sausage Chili with Cilantro (p88)
Sweet Potato Hummus (p28)
Tilapia with Italian Herbs and Vegetables (p90)
Triple Bean Salad with Basil & Garlic (p62)

GINGER

FLAVOR
Ginger is not only used in cooking but is also a wonderful way to add zing to fresh juice. Ginger has a sharp yet subtle flavor with a tangy freshness, light spiciness with a slightly sweet and refreshing taste.

AROMA
Ginger has a fresh, lemony, pungent aroma.

COOKING & FOOD PAIRING
Ginger can add zing to all types of dishes, from salads to entrees. Fresh ginger's tanginess, spiciness, warmth and sweetness complement a range of dishes, from sweet to savory. It can be a dominant flavoring, or it pairs well with other flavors. Beyond the traditional Asian dishes like stir-frys and dipping sauces, ginger is equally at home when used in cookies, biscuits, ice-cream and cakes.

HEALTH BENEFITS
Ginger is one of the oldest and most popular medicinal spices. Ginger is an excellent natural remedy for nausea, motion sickness, morning sickness and general stomach upset due to its carminative effect which helps break up and expel intestinal gas. Some studies show ginger may also help prevent certain forms of cancer. Ginger tea has been recommended to alleviate nausea in chemotherapy patients because its natural properties do not interact in a negative way with other medications.

GOURMET GARDEN GINGER
Each 4 oz. tube contains 21 pieces of finely chopped ginger and is gluten free. Find Gourmet Garden Ginger in the fresh produce section of your supermarket.

RECIPES
Cabbage Salad with Ginger & Cilantro Dressing (p40)

Coconut Ginger Tartlets with Berries (p92)

Curry Ginger Chicken Salad (p42)

Ginger Lemon Grass Asparagus (p50)

Ginger Macaroons (p90)

Ginger Snap-Awake Breakfast Cookie (p20)

Pulled Ginger-Chicken Slider with Cilantro Slaw (p84)

Pumpkin Ginger Flax and Walnut Bread (p24)

Spicy Greens and Chickpea Soup (p36)

ITALIAN HERBS

FLAVOR
Italian herb blends typically combine the flavors of basil, thyme, parsley, marjoram, rosemary and oregano. The result is a perfect blend with the aroma of a great Italian meal.

COOKING & FOOD PAIRING
Italy is known for its abundance of herbs from basil and rosemary to oregano and thyme. Italian herbs are perfect in a wide range of both traditional and modern dishes including pasta, pizza, bruschetta, salad, soups, veal and chicken.

Add Gourmet Garden Italian Herbs to your favorite spaghetti Bolognaise or meatloaf recipe for that authentic Mediterranean flavor. You can also add to butter for corn on the cob before barbecuing. Combine Italian Herbs and Garlic with balsamic vinegar and olive oil for a perfect Italian salad dressing.

HEALTH BENEFITS
A blend of the following herbs oregano, basil, marjoram, thyme, parsley & rosemary packs a powerful punch of antioxidants and anti-microbial benefits.

GOURMET GARDEN ITALIAN HERBS
Each 4 oz. tube contains 3 bunches of chopped fresh oregano, basil, marjoram, thyme, parsley & rosemary and is gluten free. Find Gourmet Garden Italian Herbs in the fresh produce section of your supermarket.

RECIPES
Barley Risotto with Italian Herbs (p66)

Beet Salad with Italian Herbs (p38)

Italian Herbs Chickpea Salad (p54)

Mixed Greens and Pears with Italian Herbs Dressing (p56)

Polenta Benedict with Italian Herb Yogurt "Hollandaise" (p22)

Tilapia with Italian Herbs and Vegetables (p90)

LEMON GRASS

FLAVOR
Lemon grass has a refreshing lemon-lime taste with a tinge of mint and ginger. While the stalk itself is too hard to eat, the soft inner part adds a tangy citron flavor to curries and stir-frys. The new leaves can be chopped and used to flavor dishes, or infused as a tea.

AROMA
Fresh lemon grass has a delicate, floral rose-like fragrance mixed with a fresh and grassy aroma.

COOKING & FOOD PAIRING
Fresh, fragrant and flavorsome, lemon grass adds body and a touch of the exotic to meals without overpowering or dominating the flavor profile of a dish. It pairs well with garlic, galangal, shallots, turmeric, ginger, chicken, pork, fish and chili peppers. Lemon grass is predominantly used in Thai, Indonesian, Vietnamese and Malaysian soups, curries, stews, Laksas, rendangs and condiments. It is very versatile and can be added to many dishes for a subtle lemon flavor and of course goes well in desserts.

HEALTH BENEFITS
Traditionally, lemon grass is used to improve blood circulation and ease muscle pain. It is also used in teas to cure loss of appetite and reduce fever. Lemon grass is considered to be a great cleanser as it can detoxify the digestive tract, bladder, kidney, pancreas and the liver. Additionally, it is thought that this herb can reduce toxins, excess fats, cholesterol while also stimulating lactation and digestion.

GOURMET GARDEN LEMON GRASS
Each 4 oz. tube contains 6 stalks of finely chopped fresh lemon grass and is gluten free. Find Gourmet Garden Lemon Grass in the fresh produce section of your supermarket.

RECIPES
Caribbean Turkey Burger with Chili Pepper Mayo (p68)

Coconut Ginger Tartlets with Berries (p92)

Ginger Lemon Grass Asparagus (p50)

Lemon Grass Pot de Crème (p96)

Spicy Greens and Chickpea Soup (p36)

Wild & Brown Rice with Lemon Grass & Parsley (p64)

OREGANO

FLAVOR
Oregano has a slightly floral and bitter taste that is both lemony and perfumy.

AROMA
Oregano has a distinct green plant and slightly lemony aroma.

COOKING & FOOD PAIRING
One of Italy's favorite herbs, oregano is a mild-flavored herb and can be used in tomato-based sauces as well as sprinkled over pizzas, pasta sauces, stews, grilled fish and kebabs. Oregano is lovely when used in moussaka and Greek-style dishes featuring feta, chicken or fish.

HEALTH BENEFITS
Oregano has the ability to treat exhaustion, nervous disorders and tension when added to a cup of tea. Oregano is a used as a traditional remedy for upset stomachs, low blood pressure, whooping cough, skin irritations, toothaches, headaches and asthma.

GOURMET GARDEN OREGANO
Each 4 oz. tube contains 3 bunches of chopped fresh oregano and is gluten free. Find Gourmet Garden Oregano in the fresh produce section of your supermarket

RECIPES
Greek Salad with Lemon Garlic Dressing (p52)

Oregano and Feta Grilled Flatbread (p32)

PARSLEY

FLAVOR
Parsley has a light and fresh grassy green flavor.

AROMA
Parsley has a grassy and slightly lemony aroma.

COOKING & FOOD PAIRING
Parsley is the perfect addition to many classic sauces, soups, stews, fish, meat, poultry, egg dishes, potatoes, salad and stuffing. Parsley is typically added toward the end of cooking as a flavor enhancement.

HEALTH BENEFITS
Parsley was historically used to treat stomach ailments and menstrual problems, arthritis and colic. Parsley is believed to maintain the elasticity of blood vessels, clean the blood and speed oxygen metabolism.

GOURMET GARDEN PARSLEY
Each 4 oz. tube contains 3 bunches of chopped fresh parsley and is gluten free. Find Gourmet Garden Parsley in the fresh produce section of your supermarket.

RECIPES
Baked Hot Wings with Bleu Cheese Parsley Dip (p26)

Basil Mushroom Frittata (p18)

Cheeseless Herbed Mac and Cheese (p70)

Cilantro Lentil Soup (p30)

Cioppino with Garlic, Basil and Parsley (p76)

Garlicky Spaghetti Squash Carbonara (p78)

Greek Salad with Lemon Garlic Dressing (p52)

Pearl Couscous with Parsley, Cilantro and Greens (p60)

Wild & Brown Rice with Lemon Grass & Parsley (p64)

BASIL MUSHROOM FRITTATA   SERVES 4

1 Tbsp olive oil

8 oz Cremini mushrooms, chopped

1 small onion, finely chopped

4 eggs

6 egg whites

1 Tbsp Gourmet Garden Basil

1 tsp Gourmet Garden Parsley

1 Tbsp Gourmet Garden Garlic

¼ tsp ground black pepper

¼ cup skim milk

½ cup shredded parmesan cheese

STEP 1

- Heat oven to 375°F. Add olive oil to a medium nonstick, oven safe skillet over medium-high heat. Add mushrooms and onions; cook until onions are tender and mushrooms are dry.

STEP 2

- In a large bowl, whisk together eggs, egg whites, Gourmet Garden Basil, Gourmet Garden Parsley, Gourmet Garden Garlic, ground black pepper and milk. Pour over the mushrooms and onions, stirring and shaking pan until large curds form. Smooth out the top of the frittata with a flat spatula. Sprinkle with parmesan cheese and put in the oven.

STEP 3

- Bake frittata for 15-20 minutes or until set and cheese is golden brown. Remove from oven and slide frittata out of the pan onto a cutting board. Slice into 8 wedges.

Per serving: 212 calories; 11g total fat; 4g saturated fat; 194 mg cholesterol; 563 mg sodium; 2g fiber; 7g carbohydrates; 17g protein

Ginger Snap Awake Breakfast Cookie

SERVES 12

½ cup brown sugar

½ cup canola oil

2 egg whites

1 tsp vanilla

½ cup natural peanut butter

½ cup no-sugar-added applesauce

2 Tbsp Gourmet Garden Ginger

1 cup whole wheat flour

2 cups old fashioned, rolled oats

1 cup bran flakes, crushed

1 tsp cinnamon

½ tsp baking soda

½ tsp salt

STEP 1
- Heat oven to 350°F. Spray a large baking sheet with cooking spray or line with parchment paper.

STEP 2
- In a medium bowl, beat brown sugar, canola oil, egg whites and vanilla together with a hand mixer or stand mixer. Add peanut butter, applesauce and Gourmet Garden Ginger; beat until smooth.

STEP 3
- In a large bowl, combine whole wheat flour, oats, bran flakes, cinnamon, baking soda, and salt. Make a well in the center of dry ingredients and pour in egg mixture. Mix wet ingredients into dry ingredients until batter is incorporated. Do not over mix.

STEP 4
- Make into 2-inch dough balls and place on cookie sheet at least an inch apart; flatten with bottom of glass or measuring cup. Bake 8-10 minutes or until slightly golden on bottom.

Tip: Store in an air tight container.

Per serving: 291 calories; 16g total fat; 2g saturated fat; 0 mg cholesterol; 229 mg sodium; 4g fiber; 32g carbohydrates; 6g protein

POLENTA BENEDICT WITH
ITALIAN HERB YOGURT HOLLANDAISE SERVES 8

1 (18 oz) pkg precooked ready to heat and serve polenta

½ cup shredded parmesan cheese

2 egg yolks

1 tsp lemon juice

¼ cup vegetable broth

1 Tbsp Gourmet Garden Italian Herb Blend

1 tsp Gourmet Garden Garlic

¼ cup non-fat, plain Greek yogurt

1 Tbsp olive oil

8 eggs, poached

¼ cup shredded parmesan

STEP 1
• Slice polenta into 8 rounds. Heat olive oil in a medium nonstick pan over medium heat. Cook each polenta slice on both sides until golden brown. Keep warm.

STEP 2
• To make the Hollandaise, prepare a double boiler using a heat proof bowl. Add egg yolks, lemon juice, vegetable broth, Gourmet Garden Italian Herb Blend and Gourmet Garden Garlic to the bowl over double boiler, whisking constantly until hot but not curdled. Remove from heat and whisk in yogurt. Keep warm.

STEP 3
• Top each polenta round with a poached egg and 2 Tbsp of the Hollandaise sauce. Sprinkle each with shredded parmesan.

Per serving: 312 calories; 10g total fat; 4g saturated fat; 238 mg cholesterol; 297 mg sodium; 5g fiber; 40g carbohydrates; 15g protein

Pumpkin Ginger Flax and Walnut Bread

YIELD: 3 LOAVES (24 SERVINGS)

2½ cups sugar

1 cup canola oil

4 eggs, beaten

1 (16 oz) can pumpkin

2 Tbsp Gourmet Garden Ginger

3 cups flour

½ cup ground flax seed

2 tsp baking soda

2 tsp salt

1 tsp baking powder

1 tsp nutmeg

1 tsp cinnamon

1 tsp allspice

½ tsp ground cloves

⅔ cup water

1 cup toasted coarsely chopped walnuts

STEP 1

- Combine sugar, oil, and eggs in bowl. Mix well. Stir in pumpkin and Gourmet Garden Ginger until blended.

STEP 2

- Sift flour, flax seed, baking soda, salt, baking powder, nutmeg, cinnamon, allspice and cloves together. Add to pumpkin mixture; mix well. Stir in water and walnuts. Pour evenly into three greased 8x4-inch loaf pans. Bake at 350°F for 50 minutes to 1 hour or until toothpick comes out clean.

Per serving: 286 calories; 14g total fat; 1g saturated fat; 31 mg cholesterol; 121 mg sodium; 2g fiber; 36g carbohydrates; 4g protein

Baked Hot Wings with Bleu Cheese Parsley Dip
SERVES 12

3 lbs chicken wings (split into wings and drumettes)

1 tsp ground black pepper

½ cup ketchup

¼ cup white wine vinegar

¼ cup honey

1 Tbsp Gourmet Garden Garlic

2 Tbsp Gourmet Garden Chili Pepper

1 Tbsp Gourmet Garden Parsley

For Dip:

1 cup non-fat, plain Greek yogurt

¼ cup crumbled bleu cheese

1 Tbsp Gourmet Garden Parsley

1 tsp Gourmet Garden Garlic

STEP 1
- Heat oven to 400°F. Coat a large baking sheet with nonstick cooking spray, season chicken wings with ground black pepper and lay in a single layer on the sheet.

STEP 2
- In a medium bowl, whisk together ketchup, white wine vinegar, honey, Gourmet Garden Garlic, Gourmet Garden Chili Pepper and Gourmet Garden Parsley. Coat chicken wings with half of the sauce and bake for 10 minutes.

STEP 3
- Coat the wings with the remaining sauce and bake for an additional 15 minutes. Remove from oven and let cool slightly before serving.

STEP 4
- While wings are baking, combine the dip ingredients in a small bowl; set aside. Serve the wings on a large platter with dipping sauce.

Per serving: 124 calories; 4g total fat; 1g saturated fat; 35 mg cholesterol; 266 mg sodium; 1g fiber; 6g carbohydrates; 14g protein

CILANTRO AND SWEET POTATO HUMMUS SERVES 8-10

CILANTRO HUMMUS

2 (15 oz) cans chickpeas, drained

1 Tube Gourmet Garden Cilantro

2 Tbsp Gourmet Garden Garlic or Chunky Garlic

2 Tbsp Olive oil

⅓ cup water

2 Tbsp lemon juice

1 tsp cumin

1 tsp Gourmet Garden Chili Pepper, optional

STEP 1

• Put all ingredients into blender or food processor. Blend until smooth. Add Gourmet Garden Chili Pepper, if desired.

STEP 2

• Serve with pita chips, pita bread or fresh vegetables.

Tip: Use leftover hummus as a sandwich spread.

Per serving: 152 calories; 6g total fat; 1g saturated fat; 0 mg cholesterol; 594 mg sodium; 7g fiber; 17g carbohydrates; 5g protein

SWEET POTATO HUMMUS

1 lb sweet potatoes (about 2), baked and peeled

1 (15 oz) can chickpeas, drained

2 Tbsp Gourmet Garden Garlic or Chunky Garlic

2 Tbsp Olive oil

⅓ cup water

2 Tbsp lemon juice

2 tsp cumin

1 tsp Gourmet Garden Chili Pepper

STEP 1

• Put all ingredients into blender or food processor. Blend until smooth. Add Gourmet Garden Chili Pepper.

STEP 2

• Serve with pita chips, pita bread or fresh vegetables.

Tip: Use leftover hummus as a sandwich spread.

Per serving: 130 calories; 5g total fat; 1g saturated fat; 0 mg cholesterol; 308 mg sodium; 4g fiber; 18g carbohydrates; 4g protein

CILANTRO LENTIL SOUP   SERVES 8

1 Tbsp olive oil

1 medium onion, chopped

1 medium carrot, peeled and chopped

1 celery stalk, chopped

1 red bell pepper, seeded and chopped

1 cup lentils

2 Tbsp Gourmet Garden Garlic

2 Tbsp Gourmet Garden Cilantro

1 Tbsp Gourmet Garden Parsley

½ tsp ground black pepper

2 quarts low sodium vegetable broth

STEP 1
Heat oil in stock pot over medium high heat. Add onion, carrot, celery and red bell pepper; cook until onion begins to turn clear, about 5 minutes.

STEP 2
Add lentils, Gourmet Garden Garlic, Gourmet Garden Cilantro, Gourmet Garden Parsley, and ground black pepper. Cook 1 more minute.

STEP 3
Add vegetable broth. Bring to a boil; reduce heat to a simmer for 25 minutes, stirring occasionally or until lentils are tender.

Per serving: 147 calories; 2g total fat; 0g saturated fat; 0 mg cholesterol; 372 mg sodium; 5g fiber; 22g carbohydrates; 6g protein

OREGANO FETA GRILLED FLATBREAD SERVES 8

1 pkg (16 oz) whole wheat pizza dough

2 Tbsp olive oil

2 Tbsp Gourmet Garden Garlic

2 Tbsp Gourmet Garden Oregano

3.5 oz reduced fat feta cheese

1 red bell pepper, roasted, peeled, seeded and thinly sliced (or substitute jarred roasted bell pepper)

1 yellow bell pepper roasted, peeled, seeded and thinly sliced (or substitute jarred roasted bell pepper)

STEP 1
- Prepare dough according to package directions. Divide into 2 pieces, roll out on a lightly floured surface.

STEP 2
- While the dough is resting, prepare an indoor or outdoor grill.

STEP 3
- Mix olive oil, Gourmet Garden Garlic, Gourmet Garden Oregano, feta cheese and roasted bell peppers in a bowl, set aside.

STEP 4
- Turn the grill heat to low; lightly brush one side of dough with olive oil and put on the grill. Grill for 3-4 minutes or until crispy on the bottom. Turn the dough over; top each dough with half the Feta pepper mixture; grill for 3-4 minutes or until crispy on the bottom. Remove from the grill. Slice & serve.

Tip: Place under the broiler for 5-6 minutes or until cheese begins to brown; if desired.

Substitute: Use Gourmet Garden Parsley in this recipe if oregano isn't available.

Per serving: 206 calories; 8g total fat; 2g saturated fat; 4 mg cholesterol; 631 mg sodium; 4g fiber; 28g carbohydrates; 7g protein

SPANISH STYLE BASIL & GREENS GAZPACHO
MAKES 8 CUPS (8 SERVINGS)

1 cup low-fat buttermilk

1 Tube Gourmet Garden Basil

2 Tbsp Gourmet Garden Garlic

¼ cup sherry vinegar, plus some for garnish

¾ cup slivered blanched almonds

½ small white onion, chopped

1 bag (13.25 oz) spinach & greens

1 large English cucumber, chopped

1 cup vegetable stock

STEP 1
- Combine all ingredients in a blender. Cover; blend until smooth. Add more stock or buttermilk if you like a thinner consistency. Chill.

STEP 2
- Serve drizzled with sherry vinegar, if desired.

Tip: Can be served immediately but flavors meld better after 1 hour chilled. Can be chilled & served for up to 24 hours.

Per serving: 120 calories; 5g total fat; 1g saturated fat; 1 mg cholesterol; 592 mg sodium; 5g fiber; 10g carbohydrates; 4g protein

SPICY GREENS AND CHICKPEA SOUP SERVES 8

1 Tbsp olive oil

1 medium onion, diced

2 quarts low sodium vegetable broth

2 cans (15 oz) chickpeas (Garbanzo Beans), drained and rinsed

1 can (14.5 oz) no-salt-added diced tomatoes

2 Tbsp Gourmet Garden Garlic

1 tsp Gourmet Garden Lemon Grass

1 tsp Gourmet Garden Ginger

½ tsp ground black pepper

1 lb bag fresh kale, coarsely chopped

STEP 1

- Add oil to a stockpot over medium high heat. Add onion; cook until it begins to caramelize slightly; about 8 minutes.

STEP 2

- Add remaining ingredients. Bring to a boil, reduce to a simmer for 20 minutes.

Tip: Remove any large stems from the kale, if necessary. Use baby kale to save time chopping.

Using Low Sodium Vegetable Broth AND No Salt Canned Chickpeas
Per serving: 194 calories; 3g total fat; 0g saturated fat; 0 mg cholesterol; 346 mg sodium; 8g fiber; 32g carbohydrates; 8g protein

BEET SALAD WITH ITALIAN HERBS   SERVES 8

2 Tbsp Gourmet Garden Italian Herbs

3 Tbsp orange juice

5 Tbsp olive oil

1 small shallot, finely chopped

2 lbs beets, cooked, peeled, sliced

½ cup crumbled goat cheese

STEP 1
- Combine first 4 ingredients in small bowl; set aside.

STEP 2
- Toss beets with dressing. Top with goat cheese. Serve.

Per serving: 171 calories; 11g total fat; 3g saturated fat; 7 mg cholesterol; 227 mg sodium; 4g fiber; 12g carbohydrates; 4g protein

CABBAGE SALAD WITH GINGER & CILANTRO DRESSING
SERVES 8

2 Tbsp Gourmet Garden Ginger

2 Tbsp Gourmet Garden Cilantro

1 Tbsp Gourmet Garden Garlic

1 tsp Gourmet Garden Chili Pepper

3 Tbsp lime juice

2 cups shredded cabbage

2 cups shredded red cabbage

1 cup cooked snap peas

2 green onions, sliced

1 can (8 oz) mandarin oranges, drained

1 (8 oz) pkg extra firm tofu, cut into 1-inch pieces

½ cup Chow Mein Noodles

STEP 1
• Combine first 5 ingredients in large bowl. Mix thoroughly.

STEP 2
• Combine all remaining ingredients except Chow Mein noodles. Toss with dressing. Top with Chow Mein noodles, if using. Serve.

Per serving: 86 calories; 2g total fat; 2g saturated fat; 2 mg cholesterol; 178 mg sodium; 3g fiber; 11g carbohydrates; 4g protein

Curry Ginger Chicken Salad   SERVES 8

½ cup non-fat, plain Greek yogurt

¼ cup reduced sugar apricot preserves

2 Tbsp Gourmet Garden Chili Pepper

2 Tbsp Gourmet Garden Ginger

1 tsp Gourmet Garden Cilantro

2 tsp sweet curry powder

1 ripe mango, peeled, seeded and diced

¼ cup raisins

¼ cup pine nuts, toasted

¼ tsp ground black pepper

3 cups shredded, cooked chicken breast

1 head bibb lettuce, cleaned and separated into leaves

STEP 1
• In a large bowl, whisk together yogurt, preserves, Gourmet Garden Chili Pepper, Gourmet Garden Ginger, Gourmet Garden Cilantro, and curry powder.

STEP 2
• Stir in remaining ingredients, mix well.

STEP 3
• Serve chicken salad on top of a lettuce leaves.

Per serving: 199 calories; 5g total fat; 1g saturated fat; 48 mg cholesterol; 206 mg sodium; 3g fiber; 17g carbohydrates; 20g protein

Dijon Dill Potato Salad SERVES 10

3 lbs medium red potatoes

1 cup non-fat, plain Greek Yogurt

½ cup low-fat mayonnaise

2 Tbsp Gourmet Garden Dill

3 scallions, finely chopped

½ tsp ground black pepper

¼ cup Dijon mustard

2 Tbsp agave nectar

STEP 1

• In a large pot, add potatoes; cover with cold water. Bring to a boil; cook until potatoes are tender but not falling apart (about 20-25 minutes). Drain and run potatoes under cold water to stop the cooking. Set aside to cool.

STEP 2

• While potatoes are cooling, in a large bowl whisk together remaining ingredients.

STEP 3

• Cut cooled potatoes into bite size piece; toss with dressing; to coat. Refrigerate for at least 30 minutes before serving.

Per serving: 165 calories; 2g total fat; 0g saturated fat; 3 mg cholesterol; 359 mg sodium; 3g fiber; 31g carbohydrates; 5g protein

DILL GREEN BEAN SALAD   SERVES 8

2 lbs green beans, trimmed

2 Tbsp Gourmet Garden Dill

2 Tbsp finely chopped sweet onion

2 Tbsp olive oil

2 Tbsp fresh lemon juice

¼ tsp lemon zest

2 tsp whole grain mustard

STEP 1

- Steam green beans until tender.

STEP 2

- Whisk remaining ingredients together in large bowl. Toss green beans with dressing.
- Serve immediately or chill and serve cold.

Per serving: 77 calories; 4g total fat; 1g saturated fat; 0 mg cholesterol; 122 mg sodium; 4g fiber; 9g carbohydrates; 2g protein

GARLICKY BRUSSELS SPROUTS SLAW   SERVES 10

1 lb fresh Brussels sprouts

¼ cup rice wine vinegar

1 Tbsp reduced sodium soy sauce

2 Tbsp honey

2 Tbsp Gourmet Garden Garlic

2 Tbsp Gourmet Garden Cilantro

¼ tsp ground black pepper

2 Tbsp olive oil

2 scallions, finely chopped

½ cup slivered almonds, toasted

3 slices turkey bacon, chopped and cooked crisp

STEP 1

- In a large pot, bring 6 cups of water to a boil. Add Brussels sprouts; cook in boiling water for 1 minute. Remove and run under cold water to stop the cooking. Dry the sprouts with a clean towel.

STEP 2

- Trim the stem on the Brussels sprouts and slice in half lengthwise. Using the slicing blade on a food processor, shred the Brussels sprouts. (You can also do this using the slicing side of a box grater or with a very sharp knife.)

STEP 3

- In a medium bowl, whisk together vinegar, soy sauce, honey, Gourmet Garden Garlic, Gourmet Garden Cilantro and black pepper.

STEP 4

- Add the shredded Brussels sprouts, toasted almonds and crisp turkey bacon to the dressing; mix well.

Per serving: 124 calories; 7g total fat; 1g saturated fat; 4 mg cholesterol; 355 mg sodium; 3g fiber; 12g carbohydrates; 4g protein

Ginger Lemon Grass Asparagus SERVES 8

½ cup rice wine vinegar

2 Tbsp Gourmet Garden Ginger

2 Tbsp sugar

2 lbs fresh asparagus

1 Tbsp Gourmet Garden Garlic

1 tsp Gourmet Garden Lemon Grass

2 Tbsp canola oil

2 tsp reduced sodium soy sauce

1 tsp Gourmet Garden Chili Pepper, optional

STEP 1

- Bring vinegar to a boil in a small saucepan; boil 8 minutes or until reduced by half. Remove from heat; stir in Gourmet Garden Ginger and sugar; set aside.

STEP 2

- Trim tough ends off asparagus. Bring a large pot of water to a boil; add asparagus; cook 3 minutes; remove from heat; drain. Cover with ice water to stop cooking; drain. Arrange on serving platter.

STEP 3

- Combine Gourmet Garden Garlic, Gourmet Garden Lemon Grass, canola oil, soy sauce and Gourmet Garden Chili Pepper, if using. Stir in reduced ginger vinegar mixture. Drizzle over asparagus. Serve.

Per serving: 95 calories; 4g total fat; 0g saturated fat; 0 mg cholesterol; 290 mg sodium; 3g fiber; 13g carbohydrates; 3g protein

GREEK SALAD WITH LEMON GARLIC DRESSING
SERVES 8

1 Tbsp Gourmet Garden Oregano

1 tsp Gourmet Garden Parsley

1 tsp Gourmet Garden Garlic

3 Tbsp lemon juice

5 Tbsp olive oil

1 Tbsp water if desired for consistency

2 cucumbers, peeled, seeded chopped

4 tomatoes, wedged or quartered

1 small red onion, sliced

4 oz feta cheese cubed

⅓ cup pitted Kalamata olives, halved

STEP 1
- Combine first 5 ingredients in a small bowl. Add water if desired.

STEP 2
- Toss cucumbers, tomatoes, red onion, feta cheese and olives with dressing. Serve immediately.

Substitute: Use Gourmet Garden Parsley in this recipe if oregano isn't available.

Per serving: 163 calories; 14g total fat; 4g saturated fat; 13 mg cholesterol; 371 mg sodium; 2g fiber; 6g carbohydrates; 3g protein

ITALIAN HERBS CHICKPEA SALAD

SERVES 10-12

Recipe courtesy of Chef Kari Underly

1 cup halved cherry tomatoes

1 English cucumber, quartered, cut into ¼-inch pieces

1 green onion, thinly sliced

1 cup pitted Kalamata olives, quartered

2 (15 oz) cans garbanzo beans (chickpeas), drained, rinsed

¼ cup fresh lemon juice

¼ cup olive oil

1 tsp Gourmet Garden Chunky Garlic

1 Tbsp Gourmet Garden Italian Herbs

1 tsp Gourmet Garden Chili Pepper, optional

STEP 1
- Place tomatoes and cucumbers in a large bowl. Add green onion, olives and garbanzo beans. Toss lightly to combine.

STEP 2
- Whisk together lemon juice, oil, Gourmet Garden Chunky Garlic, Gourmet Garden Italian Herbs and Gourmet Garden Chili Pepper. Add to vegetable mixture. Toss to combine. Serve.

Tip: If you love green onions feel free to add more to this salad.

Per serving: 174 calories; 11g total fat; 1g saturated fat; 0 mg cholesterol; 521 mg sodium; 5g fiber; 15g carbohydrates; 5g protein

MIXED GREENS AND PEARS WITH ITALIAN HERBS DRESSING SERVES 4

1 pkg (5 oz) spring salad mix or baby mixed greens

3 Tbsp canola oil

2 Tbsp balsamic vinegar

1 tsp Gourmet Garden Garlic

1 tsp Gourmet Garden Italian Herbs

2 tsp Gourmet Garden Chili Pepper

2 Tbsp crumbled gorgonzola cheese

2 Bosc or Bartlett pears, cored & sliced

¼ cup toasted walnuts

STEP 1
• Wash and chill greens.

STEP 2
• Whisk together oil, vinegar, Gourmet Garden Garlic, Gourmet Garden Italian Herbs and Gourmet Garden Chili Pepper. Toss with cheese and pears.

STEP 3
• Arrange greens on salad plates. Top with pear mixture. Sprinkle with walnuts and serve.

Tip: Use walnut oil instead of canola oil for a nuttier flavor.

Per serving: 227 calories; 16g total fat; 2g saturated fat; 5 mg cholesterol; 242 mg sodium; 5g fiber; 19g carbohydrates; 3g protein

Pear and Brown Rice Salad with Basil & Garlic SERVES 8-10

⅓ cup red wine vinegar

½ cup olive oil

2 Tbsp Gourmet Garden Basil

1 Tbsp Gourmet Garden Garlic

2 cups cooked long grain brown rice

3 green onions, sliced

4 Bosc or Bartlett pears, cored and chopped

½ cup toasted chopped pecans or walnuts

⅓ cup crumbled blue cheese

STEP 1
- Whisk together vinegar, oil, Gourmet Garden Basil and Gourmet Garden Garlic.

STEP 2
- Combine rice, green onions, pears and nuts. Toss with dressing to coat. Top with cheese. Serve.

Tip: Serve over lettuce leaves, if desired.

Per serving: 305 calories; 21g total fat; 3g saturated fat; 4 mg cholesterol; 218 mg sodium; 5g fiber; 27g carbohydrates; 4g protein

Pearl Couscous with Parsley, Cilantro and Greens SERVES 10

3 Tbsp lemon juice

1 Tbsp Gourmet Garden Parsley

1 Tbsp Gourmet Garden Cilantro

5 Tbsp olive oil

1 pkg (8 oz) pearl couscous
(1¾ cups-uncooked)

2 pkg (5 oz each) baby greens,
spinach or kale

1 cup shredded (or cubed)
cooked chicken

½ cup toasted pine nuts
(or slivered almonds)

4 oz crumbled goat cheese or feta

2 green onions, thinly sliced

½ cup dried cherries

STEP 1
- Combine lemon juice, Gourmet Garden Cilantro and Gourmet Garden Parsley in large bowl. Whisk in olive oil until well mixed.

STEP 2
- Make couscous according to package directions. When cooked, stir into dressing. Add greens so they wilt slightly from the heat of the couscous. Add remaining ingredients. Stir to combine.

Tip: If dried cherries are large they can be coarsely chopped for better distribution.

Per serving: 274 calories; 15g total fat; 4g saturated fat; 10 mg cholesterol; 151 mg sodium; 3g fiber; 27g carbohydrates; 7g protein

TRIPLE BEAN SALAD WITH BASIL & GARLIC SERVES 8

2 tsp Gourmet Garden Basil

1 tsp Gourmet Garden Garlic

2 Tbsp white balsamic vinegar

3 Tbsp olive oil

1 Tbsp finely chopped shallots

1 lb green beans, trimmed, blanched

8 oz edamame, thawed

8 oz snap peas, trimmed, blanched

STEP 1

• Combine first 5 ingredients in small bowl.

STEP 2

• Toss dressing with green beans, edamame and snap peas. Serve.

Per serving: 111 calories; 6g total fat; 1g saturated fat; 0 mg cholesterol; 53 mg sodium; 5g fiber; 9g carbohydrates; 6g protein

WILD & BROWN RICE WITH LEMON GRASS & PARSLEY

SERVES 8

1 cup uncooked short grain brown rice

¾ cup uncooked wild rice

1 cup dried cherries

½ cup pine nuts, toasted

3 Tbsp Gourmet Garden Lemon Grass

2 Tbsp Gourmet Garden Parsley

¾ cup cranberry juice

STEP 1

- Bring 2 cups water to a boil; add brown rice; cover; reduce heat. Cook 45 minutes. Drain any excess water. Transfer to a large bowl.

STEP 2

- Meanwhile bring 3 cups water to a boil; add wild rice; cover; simmer until tender about 45 minutes. Drain; transfer to bowl with brown rice.

STEP 3

- Add remaining ingredients; toss to combine.

STEP 4

- Transfer to an ovenproof casserole or baking dish; cover tightly with aluminum foil, bake at 350°F for 40 minutes or until heated through.

Tip: Can be made 1-2 days ahead and baked or reheated on the day you plan to serve.

Per serving: 245 calories; 6g total fat; 0g saturated fat; 0 mg cholesterol; 200 mg sodium; 4g fiber; 40g carbohydrates; 5g protein

BARLEY RISOTTO WITH ITALIAN HERBS SERVES 6

6 cups reduced sodium, fat-free chicken broth

3 tsp olive oil, divided

1 small onion, diced (1 cup)

1 cup barley

2 medium zucchini, diced

1 Tbsp Gourmet Garden Garlic

1 Tbsp Gourmet Garden Italian Herb Blend

¼ tsp ground black pepper

¼ cup grated parmesan cheese

STEP 1
- In a sauce pan, bring chicken broth to a simmer over medium heat. Keep warm on low heat.

STEP 2
- Add 1 tsp olive oil to another medium saucepan over medium heat. Add onions; cook 5 minutes or until clear. Add barley; cook 2 more minutes.

STEP 3
- Ladle about one cup of hot broth into barley mixture, stirring constantly, until liquid is absorbed. Continue one ladle at a time until the barley is cooked and has a creamy texture.

STEP 4
- Add remaining olive oil to a medium skillet over medium-high heat. Add zucchini; cook until tender. Add Gourmet Garden Garlic and Gourmet Garden Italian Herb Blend; cook 1 more minute. Add zucchini to barley mixture, with ground black pepper and parmesan cheese. Mix well. Serve immediately.

Tip: If the barley risotto gets too thick, add more hot broth, stirring, until creamy.

Per serving: 219 calories; 5g total fat; 1g saturated fat; 3 mg cholesterol; 272 mg sodium; 7g fiber; 33g carbohydrates; 10g protein

CARIBBEAN TURKEY BURGER WITH CHILI PEPPER MAYO
SERVES 4

4 pineapple rings (fresh or canned)

1 lb 93% Lean ground turkey

¼ cup old fashioned rolled oats

1 Tbsp Gourmet Garden Garlic

1 Tbsp Gourmet Garden Cilantro

2 Tbsp Gourmet Garden Chili Pepper

2 tsp Gourmet Garden Lemon Grass

½ tsp ground black pepper

1 egg

¼ cup lowfat mayonnaise

1 tsp Gourmet Garden Chili Pepper

4 butter lettuce leaves

4 slices tomato

4 whole wheat buns, optional

STEP 1

- Heat indoor or outdoor grill. When using an outdoor grill, lay a piece of foil that has been sprayed with cooking spray on the grates when you grill the burgers. Lightly spray both sides of the pineapple rings with cooking spray and grill for 2 minutes on each side; set aside.

STEP 2

- Combine ground turkey, oats, Gourmet Garden Garlic, Gourmet Garden Cilantro, 2 Tbsp Gourmet Garden Chili Pepper, Gourmet Garden Lemon Grass, ground black pepper and egg in large bowl; mix well. Divide meat mixture into 4 evenly sized patties.

STEP 3

- Lay burgers on the prepared foil on the grill. Grill for 5-6 minutes on each side or until the internal temperature of the burger reaches 165°F.

STEP 4

- In a small bowl, combine mayonnaise and 1 tsp Gourmet Garden Chili Pepper. Build each burger starting with the lettuce, burger, grilled pineapple ring, and tomato. Spoon the chili pepper mayo on top.

Tip: Serve on whole wheat buns, if desired.

Per serving: 326 calories; 15g total fat; 3g saturated fat; 139 mg cholesterol; 766 mg sodium; 4g fiber; 19g carbohydrates; 26g protein

CHEESELESS HERBED MAC AND "CHEESE" SERVES 16

1 medium butternut squash

1 pkg (13.25 oz) whole grain or whole wheat elbow macaroni

1 Tbsp olive oil

2 Tbsp flour

1 cup skim milk

2 Tbsp Gourmet Garden Garlic

2 Tbsp Gourmet Garden Basil

1 Tbsp Gourmet Garden Parsley

For Topping

1 Tbsp olive oil

1 Tbsp Gourmet Garden Garlic

1 Tbsp Gourmet Garden Parsley

½ cup whole wheat breadcrumbs

½ cup ground almonds

STEP 1

- Heat oven to 375°F. Cut butternut squash in half lengthwise, scoop out the seeds and place cut side down in a baking dish. Add ½ cup water to the baking dish and bake for 45 minutes or until squash is tender. Leave oven on after squash is done baking.

STEP 2

- Cook pasta according to package directions, omit the salt. Drain and set aside.

STEP 3

- In the same pot used to cook the pasta, add olive oil over medium heat. Add flour and cook 1 to 2 minutes to form a paste. Whisk in skim milk, Gourmet Garden Garlic, Gourmet Garden Basil and Gourmet Garden Parsley. Once squash is finished cooking, scoop the flesh out of the skin and add to the milk mixture. Using an immersion or stand up blender, puree the squash and milk mixture. Add the cooked pasta to the squash puree and stir to combine.

STEP 4

- In a small bowl, combine the topping ingredients, mix well. Coat a square or round baking dish with cooking spray. Spoon macaroni and squash mixture into the pan. Sprinkle with the topping mixture and bake for 10 minutes or until heated through and browned on top.

Per serving: 178 calories; 4g total fat; 0g saturated fat; 0 mg cholesterol; 212 mg sodium; 4g fiber; 30g carbohydrates; 6g protein

Chicken Quesadillas with Cilantro and Garlic

SERVES 8

1 Tbsp olive oil

¼ cup fresh lime juice

2 Tbsp Gourmet Garden Cilantro

1 Tbsp Gourmet Garden Garlic

1 Tbsp Gourmet Garden Chili Pepper, optional

1 lb (4-4 oz) boneless skinless chicken breasts

16 corn tortillas

2 tomatoes, thinly sliced

2 ripe avocados

4 cups shredded iceberg or romaine lettuce

½ cup non-fat plain Greek yogurt, optional

STEP 1

- Heat oven to 350°F. Whisk together olive oil, lime juice, Gourmet Garden Cilantro, Gourmet Garden Garlic and Gourmet Garden Chili Pepper, if using.

STEP 2

- Spray a 9x13 baking dish with cooking spray; add chicken breasts. Brush chicken with herb mixture. Bake for 35 minutes or until chicken reaches an internal temperature of 165°F. Remove chicken; let it rest covered with foil for 10 minutes, thinly slice.

STEP 3

- Meanwhile spray large skillet with cooking spray over medium heat. Make quesadillas by laying a corn tortilla in the pan, add 1 slice of cheese, tomato slices, ½ a sliced chicken breast, then another corn tortilla. Use a spatula to press down on quesadilla without letting ingredients spill out. Cook 2-3 minutes; flip and cook 2-3 more minutes. Repeat with remaining quesadillas.

STEP 4

- Slice quesadillas into quarters and top with ½ cup shredded lettuce, ¼ sliced avocado and 1 Tbsp non-fat greek yogurt (optional).

Per serving: 313 calories; 12g total fat; 2g saturated fat; 36 mg cholesterol; 229 mg sodium; 8g fiber; 33g carbohydrates; 19g protein

Cilantro-Honey Glazed Salmon   SERVES 4

¼ cup freshly squeezed lime juice

¼ cup olive oil

¼ cup honey

2 Tbsp Gourmet Garden Cilantro

2 Tbsp Gourmet Garden Garlic

½ tsp ground black pepper

1 lb skinless salmon filets
(4-4 oz filets)

STEP 1
- Heat oven to 375°F. Coat a baking sheet with cooking spray, set aside.

STEP 2
- In a small bowl, whisk together lime juice, olive oil, honey, Gourmet Garden Cilantro, Gourmet Garden Garlic and ground black pepper.

STEP 3
- Lay salmon filets skin side down on the prepared baking sheet. Pour ½ of the sauce over the salmon and bake for 10 minutes. Pour remaining sauce over the salmon and bake 5 more minutes. Switch oven to broil.

STEP 4
- Broil salmon for 3 minutes. When serving, spoon any extra sauce from pan over the salmon.

Per serving: 229 calories; 14g total fat; 2g saturated fat; 3 mg cholesterol; 345 mg sodium; 2g fiber; 21g carbohydrates; 1g protein

CIOPPINO WITH GARLIC, BASIL AND PARSLEY

1 Tbsp olive oil

1 medium onion, diced

1 red bell pepper, seeded and cut into 1" chunks

2 medium zucchini, cut into 1" chunks

2 Tbsp Gourmet Garden Garlic

2 Tbsp Gourmet Garden Basil, divided

2 Tbsp Gourmet Garden Parsley, divided

½ tsp ground black pepper

1 (28 oz) can no salt added crushed tomatoes

2 cups low sodium vegetable broth

8 oz cod filet, cut into 1" chunks

1 lb large shrimp, peeled and deveined

STEP 1
- Add oil to a soup pot over medium high heat. Add onion, red bell pepper and zucchini and sauté until onion begins to turn clear.

STEP 2
- Stir in Gourmet Garden Garlic, 1 Tbsp Gourmet Garden Basil, 1 Tbsp Gourmet Garden Parsley, and ground black pepper; cook for 1 more minute

STEP 3
- Add crushed tomato and vegetable broth. Bring stew to a boil, then reduce to a simmer for 15 minutes or until zucchini is tender.

STEP 4
- Stir in cod and shrimp and cook for 5 more minutes or until both are cooked through. Remove stew from heat, then stir in remaining 1 Tbsp Gourmet Garden Basil and 1 Tbsp Gourmet Garden Parsley and serve.

Per serving: 161 calories; 4g total fat; 1g saturated fat; 131 mg cholesterol; 895 mg sodium; 3g fiber; 9g carbohydrates; 19g protein

GARLICKY SPAGHETTI SQUASH CARBONARA SERVES 8

1 medium spaghetti squash

1/2 cup skim milk

5 oz silken tofu

¼ cup parmesan cheese, grated

¼ tsp ground black pepper

1 Tbsp Gourmet Garden Garlic

1 Tbsp Gourmet Garden Parsley

1 Tbsp Gourmet Garden Basil

7 slices turkey bacon, diced and cooked crisp

STEP 1

- Heat oven to 400°F. Cut ends off squash then cut in half lengthwise. Scoop out seeds; wash and dry both sides. Coat a baking dish with cooking spray. Place squash halves face down in baking dish; spray the skins lightly with cooking spray. Bake 40 minutes then remove squash meat from rind, scraping and pulling with fork into strands and place in a medium serving bowl. Set aside; keep warm.

STEP 2

- In a small sauce pan, combine skim milk, tofu, parmesan cheese and ground black pepper. Bring to a simmer then blend in a blender. Return to the pan and stir in the Gourmet Garden Garlic, Gourmet Garden Parsley and Gourmet Garden Basil. Cook for 1 more minute.

STEP 3

- Ladle sauce on top of squash, then sprinkle with turkey bacon.

Per serving: 84 calories; 4g total fat; 1g saturated fat; 11 mg cholesterol; 422 mg sodium; 2g fiber; 6g carbohydrates; 5g protein

Multigrain Spaghetti with Basil Kale Pesto

SERVES 6

¾ lb kale, stemmed, rinsed

½ cup whole raw almonds

1 Tube Gourmet Garden Basil

2 Tbsp Gourmet Garden Garlic

¼ cup olive oil

½ cup water

¼ cup shredded parmesan

8 oz multigrain spaghetti

STEP 1

- Bring large pot of water to boil. Submerge all kale in boiling water, stirring until bright green but still crisp; 60-90 seconds. Drain kale; rinse with cold water to stop cooking. Squeeze dry.

STEP 2

- In blender or food processor; combine kale, almonds, Gourmet Garden Basil, Gourmet Garden Garlic, oil and water. Blend until smooth. Add cheese. Blend. Add more water, if necessary, to reach desired consistency.

STEP 3

- Cook 8 oz. multigrain spaghetti according to package directions. Drain; toss immediately with ¾ cup basil kale pesto. Serve immediately.

STEP 4

- Reserve remaining pesto for another use. Pesto will keep in an airtight container in refrigerator for 1-2 weeks. Can be frozen for up to 6 months. Makes 1½ cups.

Per serving: 359 calories; 17g total fat; 2g saturated fat; 2 mg cholesterol; 599 mg sodium; 10g fiber; 40g carbohydrates; 11g protein

PENNE WITH GARLIC, CHICKEN, BASIL AND GREENS

SERVES 8

1 Tbsp olive oil

½ small onion, finely chopped

1 pkg (8 oz) sliced wild mushrooms

1 Tbsp Gourmet Garden Basil

1 Tbsp Gourmet Garden Garlic

1 tsp Gourmet Garden Chili Pepper

1½ cups (8 oz) shredded chicken

1 cup low sodium chicken broth

1 pkg (5 oz) spinach or baby kale

1 cup grape tomatoes

8 oz uncooked multigrain or whole wheat pasta

¼ cup shredded parmesan cheese, optional

STEP 1

- Add olive oil to a large skillet over medium-high heat. Add onions and mushrooms; cook until onions are tender and mushrooms are dry. Stir in Gourmet Garden Basil, Gourmet Garden Garlic and Gourmet Garden Chili Pepper; cook 1 minute. Add chicken, broth, spinach or kale and tomatoes; bring to a boil; reduce heat. Keep warm.

STEP 2

- Meanwhile cook pasta according to package directions. Drain; reserving ½ cup pasta water.

STEP 3

- Add cooked drained pasta to skillet with chicken and vegetable mixture. Toss well. If pasta seems dry add reserved pasta water. Serve topped with parmesan.

Per serving: 201 calories; 4g total fat; 1g saturated fat; 24 mg cholesterol; 186 mg sodium; 4g fiber; 26g carbohydrates; 14g protein

PULLED GINGER-CHICKEN SLIDER WITH CILANTRO SLAW SERVES 8

1½ lbs boneless skinless
chicken thighs

1 lb boneless skinless chicken breasts

1 small onion, finely chopped

2 Tbsp Gourmet Garden Ginger

1 Tbsp Gourmet Garden Garlic

1 cup ketchup

2 Tbsp dark brown sugar

¼ cup lime juice, divided

2 Tbsp olive oil

1 Tbsp Gourmet Garden Cilantro

2 cups shredded red cabbage

½ cup finely sliced red onion

16 whole wheat slider buns

STEP 1
- Add first 7 ingredients and 2 Tbsp lime juice to the slow cooker, cover and put on high for 6 hours.

STEP 2
- When chicken is done, remove from sauce and shred. Return to sauce. Keep warm.

STEP 3
- Meanwhile combine 2 Tbsp lime juice, olive oil and Gourmet Garden Cilantro in a medium bowl. Toss with red cabbage and red onion.

STEP 4
- Divide chicken and red cabbage slaw evenly among 16 whole wheat slider buns. Serve.

Per serving: 358 calories; 11g total fat; 2g saturated fat; 94 mg cholesterol; 672 mg sodium; 5g fiber; 38g carbohydrates; 28g protein

Slow Cooker Cilantro Shredded Beef (Ropa Vieja) SERVES 10

2 lbs flank steak

2 red bell peppers, seeded and sliced

1 large red onion, sliced

1 tube Gourmet Garden Cilantro

2 Tbsp Gourmet Garden Garlic

2 Tbsp Gourmet Garden Chili Pepper

1 (15 oz) can, no salt added, diced tomatoes

½ cup red wine vinegar

½ tsp ground black pepper

1 Tbsp ground cumin

STEP 1
- Add all ingredients to the slow cooker, cover and put on high for 6 hours.

STEP 2
- When the meat is done, remove from the sauce and shred.

STEP 3
- Return shredded meat to the sauce. Serve with a salad or corn tortillas.

Per serving: 181 calories; 5g total fat; 2g saturated fat; 53 mg cholesterol; 393 mg sodium; 3g fiber; 8g carbohydrates; 20g protein

Spicy Turkey Sausage Chili with Cilantro

SERVES 8

1 Tbsp olive oil

1 large chopped onion

1 red pepper, stemmed & chopped

1 lb Italian turkey sausage, cut into chunks

4 oz sliced mushrooms

2 Tbsp Gourmet Garden Garlic

2 (15 oz) cans low sodium black beans, drained

1 (14.5 oz) can no salt diced tomatoes, undrained

1 Tbsp Gourmet Garden Chili Pepper

3 Tbsp Gourmet Garden Cilantro

1 tsp ground cumin

Optional Garnishes:

2 green onions, sliced

¼ cup fat-free (0%) Greek yogurt

STEP 1

- Heat oil, add onions and red pepper, cook 5 minutes. Add sausage and mushrooms, cook about 5 minutes (until lightly browned).

STEP 2

- Add Gourmet Garden Garlic, beans, tomatoes, Gourmet Garden Chili Pepper and Gourmet Garden Cilantro; heat to a boil. Reduce heat to low. Simmer until vegetables are tender about 10–15 minutes. Serve topped with green onions and yogurt, if desired.

Per serving: 237 calories; 8g total fat; 2g saturated fat; 30 mg cholesterol; 662 mg sodium; 8g fiber; 26g carbohydrates; 16g protein

TILAPIA WITH ITALIAN HERBS AND VEGETABLES

SERVES 4

2 tsp olive oil, divided

8 oz mushrooms, sliced

1 Tbsp Gourmet Garden Garlic

1 cup grape or small cherry tomatoes

3 green onions, thinly sliced

3 Tbsp Gourmet Garden Italian Herbs

4 (6 oz) Tilapia Filets

STEP 1

- Heat 1 tsp olive oil in skillet. Add mushrooms; cook 4 minutes to release liquid. Add tomatoes and Gourmet Garden Garlic; cook 5 minutes or until tomatoes start to soften. Add snap peas, cover; cook 5 minutes or until snap peas turn bright green and are tender. Stir in green onions. Remove vegetables from skillet; keep warm.

STEP 2

- Coat fish filets evenly on both sides with Gourmet Garden Italian Herbs. Heat remaining olive oil in skillet. Add fish; cook 3 minutes per side; in two batches if necessary.

STEP 3

- Serve with warm vegetables.

Per serving: 228 calories; 6g total fat; 1g saturated fat; 65 mg cholesterol; 460 mg sodium; 38g fiber; 6g carbohydrates; 32g protein

COCONUT GINGER TARTLETS WITH BERRIES SERVES 9

14 oz sweetened shredded coconut

4 egg whites

1 tsp Gourmet Garden Ginger

¼ cup honey

2 tsp Gourmet Garden Lemon Grass

4 cups mixed fresh berries
(strawberry, raspberry, blueberry,
blackberry)

STEP 1
• Heat oven to 350°F. Coat 9 non-stick muffin pan cups with cooking spray, set aside.

STEP 2
• In a medium bowl, mix together coconut, egg whites and Gourmet Garden Ginger, stirring well. Divide the coconut mixture evenly among the 9 muffin cups and press down and up the sides to form a crust. Bake for 15-20 minutes until golden brown and cooked through. Remove from oven and using a spoon, press down the bottom of the crust if puffed up. Cool completely before removing from muffin pan.

STEP 3
• Meanwhile combine honey and Gourmet Garden Lemon Grass in a large bowl; toss with berries; refrigerate for 1 hour.

STEP 4
• When tartlets are cool, remove from pan. Fill with berry mixture dividing it evenly among them.

Per serving: 291 calories; 16g total fat; 14g saturated fat; 0 mg cholesterol; 170 mg sodium; 5g fiber; 36g carbohydrates; 4g protein

GINGER MACAROONS SERVES 9

14 oz sweetened shredded coconut

5 egg whites

1 Tbsp Gourmet Garden Ginger

2 oz Semi-sweet chocolate

STEP 1

- Heat oven to 325°F. Coat a baking sheet with cooking spray. Set aside.

STEP 2

- In a medium bowl, mix together coconut, egg whites and Gourmet Garden Ginger, stirring well. Using a 2-inch scoop, scoop coconut mixture, packing tightly, into balls, place about 1 inch apart on baking sheet. Bake for 45 minutes or until outside of coconut is golden brown.

STEP 3

- While macaroons are baking, melt chocolate over a double boiler or in a microwave. Keep warm.

STEP 4

- Remove macaroons from oven and let cool slightly. Once slightly cooled, drizzle with chocolate.

Per serving: 263 calories; 18g total fat; 15g saturated fat; 0 mg cholesterol; 149 mg sodium; 3g fiber; 26g carbohydrates; 4g protein

LEMON GRASS POT DE CREME SERVES 8

2 tsp powdered gelatin

2 Tbsp cold water

1 cup skim milk

1 tsp Gourmet Garden Ginger

2 Tbsp Gourmet Garden Lemon Grass

1 tsp vanilla

⅓ cup agave nectar

½ cup low fat buttermilk

1 cup non-fat, plain Greek yogurt

1 Tbsp fresh lime juice

Lime zest as needed

STEP 1
- Mix gelatin and cold water in a small bowl and set aside to bloom.

STEP 2
- In a medium-sized pot, begin warming skim milk, Gourmet Garden Ginger, Gourmet Garden Lemon Grass and vanilla. As it's heating, quickly whisk in the bloomed gelatin when milk starts to bubble around the edges, remove pot from heat and set aside. Do not boil.

STEP 3
- In a large mixing bowl, whisk together agave nectar, buttermilk, yogurt and lime juice. Once the milk mixture has cooled slightly, add it to the mixing bowl, whisking well to combine. Strain through a fine mesh sieve and divide mixture into 4 oz. ramekins or martini glasses. Top with lime zest to taste.

STEP 4
- Place ramekins or glasses in the refrigerator to chill for at least 3-4 hours. Overnight is best.

Per serving: 87 calories; 1g total fat; 0g saturated fat; 1 mg cholesterol; 137 mg sodium; 1g fiber; 14g carbohydrates; 5g protein

SAMPLE MEAL PLAN
for healthy living

Approximately 1500 calories/day

	MONDAY	TUESDAY	WEDNESDAY
Breakfast	2 Ginger Snap Awake Breakfast Cookies; 1 cup skim or vanilla almond milk	1 slice Pumpkin Ginger Flax and Walnut Bread; 1 cup skim or vanilla almond milk	Basil Mushroom Frittata; 1 whole grain English muffin
Lunch	1 cup Curry Ginger Chicken Salad; Iced Green Tea with honey and lemon; Apple	Cilantro Lentil Soup; 1 whole grain dinner roll	1 cup Pear and Brown Rice Salad with Basil & Garlic; 4 oz. canned tuna; Iced Green Tea with honey and lemon; Apple
Snack	1/4 cup Cilantro Hummus and 10 baked pita chips	1 Ginger Snap Awake Breakfast Cookie and 4 oz non-fat Greek yogurt (dip your cookie in the yogurt)	1 slice Pumpkin Ginger Flax and Walnut Bread; 1 cup Hot Green Tea
Dinner	Tilapia with Italian Herbs and Vegetables; 1 cup Greek Salad with Lemon Garlic Dressing	Slow Cooker Cilantro Shredded Beef (Ropa Vieja) with 2 corn tortillas; Small green salad	1 cup cold Slow Cooker Cilantro Shredded Beef (Ropa Vieja) mixed with 2 cups salad greens, 1 cup diced tomatoes and 1 cup diced cucumber
Dessert			
Tips	*Make the Ginger Snap Awake Breakfast Cookies ahead of time and freeze them. When you're ready for breakfast, thaw them in the microwave for 1 minute and you're out the door with a hot breakfast!*	*Get all of your ingredients ready the night before and then start the slow cooker before you leave for work. When you get home, dinner is served!*	*Make your frittata when you are cooking dinner the night before, portion it into a microwave-safe container, and heat and serve in the morning.*

THURSDAY	FRIDAY	SATURDAY	SUNDAY
2 Ginger Snap Awake Breakfast Cookies; 1 cup skim or vanilla almond milk	1 slice Pumpkin Ginger Flax and Walnut Bread; Apple	Basil Mushroom Frittata; 1 cup cubed cantaloupe; 1 whole grain English muffin	Polenta Benedict with Italian Herb Yogurt Hollandaise; 1 cup mixed berries
1 grilled chicken breast (cold and sliced) over 1 cup Greek Salad with Lemon Garlic Dressing	Cold Cilantro-Honey Glazed Salmon tossed with mixed salad greens	Spicy Turkey Sausage Chili with Cilantro; 1 whole grain dinner roll	1 grilled chicken breast; Garlicky Brussels Sprouts Slaw; Iced Green Tea with honey and lemon
1 cup Spanish Style Basil & Greens Gazpacho	1/2 cup Sweet Potato Hummus with 12 baked tortilla chips	Lemon Grass Pot de Créme; 1 cup mixed berries	1/2 cup Sweet Potato Hummus with 1 cup mixed raw vegetables
Cilantro-Honey Glazed Salmon with Garlicky Brussels Sprouts Slaw	Spicy Turkey Sausage Chili with Cilantro; Pearl Couscous with Parsley, Cilantro and Greens; 4 oz Red or White wine	Dinner out!	Cioppino with Garlic, Basil and Parsley; 1 whole grain roll; Small green salad
	Lemon Grass Pot de Créme		Lemon Grass Pot de Créme
The Spanish Style Basil & Greens Gazpacho is a great go-to snack to always keep handy in your refrigerator. You eat it cold, so there's no reheating or even silverware needed. Just drink it cold right out of your pre-portioned container!	*Friday night is treat night! Splurge with a glass of wine and a little guilt-free dessert. You can make the Lemon Grass Pot de Créme the night before or in the morning so they are set up and ready for after dinner.*	*Do your weekly grocery shopping today and treat yourself to dinner out. If you'd rather stay home, check out all of your leftovers and have a little leftover buffet.*	*Take all of those groceries you bought yesterday and get your prep done for the week. Bake off Breakfast Cookies and freeze them. Chop and bag vegetables in portions for your lunches and portion out snacks like pita chips or tortilla chips.*

INDEX OF RECIPES BY HERB